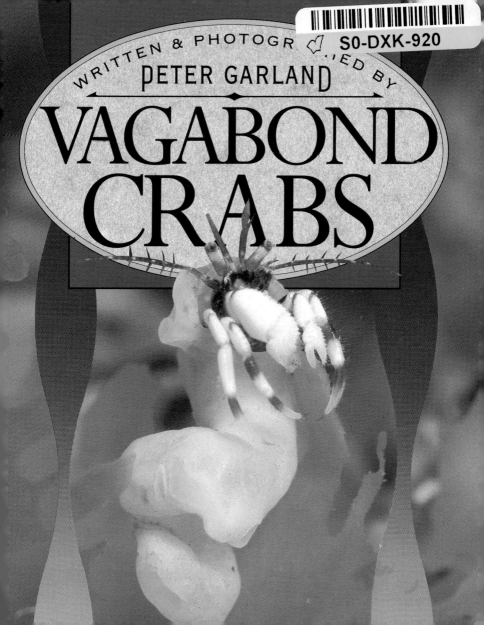

WRITTEN & PHOTOGRAPHED BY

PETER GARLAND

VAGABOND CRABS

A hermit crab found
an empty shell.
She tried it on,
it fit her well.

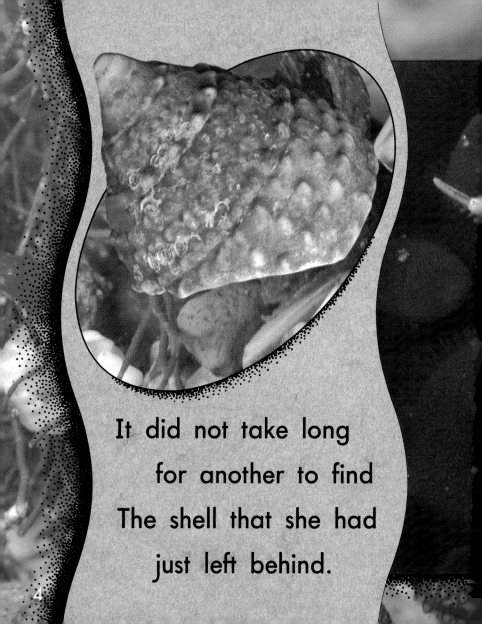

It did not take long
    for another to find
The shell that she had
    just left behind.

In and out, in and out,
along the shore,

Each shell is bigger
than the one before.

Will they always be drifting
and shifting address,

These vagabond crabs
in their fancy dress?

ABOUT HERMIT CRABS

Hermit crabs live
in pools along
the seashore.

For protection, they
live in the empty shells
of dead shellfish.

When they grow
too big for one shell,
they leave it for another.

The hermit crab's big
right claw becomes
its lid when it pulls back
into its shell for safety.